Woman on the
Edge
of Age

Eva Mewes

Eva L. Mewes

Monarch Tree
PUBLISHING

Eau Claire, Wisconsin

Woman on the Edge of Age
Copyright 2008 by Eva Mewes

Published by Monarch Tree Publishing, P. O. Box 387, Eau Claire, Wisconsin 54702-0387. (888) 895-7166.
First printing 2008.

ISBN 0-9785698-7-3

Library of Congress Control Number: 2008934189

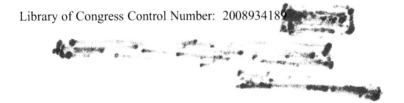

Attention organizations and educational institutions:
Quantity discounts are available on bulk purchases of this book for educational purposes or fund raising. For information, please contact Monarch Tree Publishing,
P. O. Box 387, Eau Claire, Wisconsin 54702-0387.
(888) 895-7166. Fax: (715) 874-6766. www.monarchtreepublishing.com
info@monarchtreepublishing.com

To my kids
who treat me much better than I deserve
and
the Chippewa Valley Writers
who are a great source of inspiration
and
Marge Barrett and
Linda Larkin
for all their help and encouragement.

To Elizabeth and Sharon
at Monarch Tree Publishing:
thanks, thanks, thanks.

Contents

Contents

Part 4 Who Folded This Map, Anyway?

Baby Eva with her parents.

Part 1

Where I Am From

Grandpa and Grandma
Grabow

Great-Grandparents
Elizabeth and John Nelson

Where I Am From

I am from the high plains of Europe
transplanted to the Midwest
by daring farmers
lusting after land.

I am from a world
of square, white houses,
tall, red barns, warm
with animal heat,
pungent with the smells
of silage, manure, and hay.

From small places, cozy kitchens,
one-room country schools,
sleepy villages, county fairs.

I am from a world all of one piece,
from childhood to womanhood,
from parent's home to husband's house,
from motherhood to widowhood.

I am from strong women
with rough hands and tender touch,
unafraid of endless chores,
and starting over.

John,
Elizabeth,
Ann, and
Great-Aunt
Mary.

Great-Aunt Mary

Even though her white shirt-waist
with wide leg-o-mutton sleeves
buttons demurely at her throat,
and her brown-gold hair
is coiled neatly at the nape of her neck,
you can see the sparkle
in her Dane-blue eyes.
Her mouth is wide, and her smile eager.
Her hair when loosened
ripples down her back and curls at the ends.

Some man will loosen
that hair, and she will give herself to him
in a hidden room where
the secret of their love must stay.

But fate is a hard-eyed bitch
who hates the joys of lovers,
and the unthinkable happens.
Her stern old-country father
turns his back and won't speak.
Her mother speaks often and piously,
on and on, until the child is born,
a chubby, laughing boy.

She loves this child. . . and yet,
her married lover calls her back.
Back to the passion and the ecstasy
and the joy of being fully alive.

When the seed of conception grows again,
she laces it cruelly and painfully
until she grows pale and hollow-eyed,
until something bursts inside,
For as her mother said over and over,
"The wages of sin are death!"

Nanie and a young Eva.

Nanie Cooking

Nanie doesn't measure, tosses
ingredients haphazardly, mixes
with her bare hands. The batter
rich with butter, eggs, and cream,
is a sensual experience for her.

Short, round, firmly girdled,
white curls confined in a hairnet,
light sparkling from the golden
rims of her glasses, she bustles
from cupboard to stove to table.

Tension hangs over her kitchen
like thunderheads building to a storm.
Pots and pans bang and slam,
occasionally flying across
the room when she is displeased.
Dirty dishes accumulate in her wake
like debris after a tornado.

She willingly shares her recipes,
but my efforts never taste the same.
Mother says she leaves ingredients
out on purpose, but I think
it is a lack of that electrical
energy that has left
my cooking flat.

As a young man, Bampie at a picnic in the 1920's.

In later years, Bampie taking a break from the garden.

Bampie

My Bampie was a steadfast man.
Kindly Dane-blue eyes
rested with delight
on the three generations
of children he bounced
on his knee. He sang
Every Time I Go To Town,
and a Danish folk song,
Rea, Rea, Ronka. They ended
with laughs and hugs,
and every child felt
loved and accepted.

He was a baggage man
on the railroad for
forty-seven years.
For his retirement
his friends each
put one penny
in his battered blue
enamel cup, and it came
back overflowing.

He was married to Nanie
for sixty years. They raised
five solid citizens. "My kids
never gave me a bit of trouble!"
he said in later years. A bit
of fiction that they all cherished.

Hospitalized weeks before
their sixtieth anniversary,
he told the nurses, "Be sure
you get me home for the party.
It means so much to my wife."
He died the evening
after the party,
faithful to the end.

Grandma Carrie and Kathy.

Three generations: Carrie, Kathy, and
Minnie holding Gene.

Grandma Carrie

She came to the city to help
when we had our second child.
It was how she spent her days
going from family to family
as they needed her. She cooked,
cleaned the house,
and loved the children.

Vicks and Bengay were her scents.
Her hair, suspiciously black,
was skinned into a tight
little bun on the back of her head.
Nearing eighty, she had
a dried-apple face, and wore
shapeless dresses always
covered by a bibbed apron.

She was a fervent watcher
of soap operas, and often
confused those stories
with the network news,
giving her a delightfully wacky
world vision. Her stories
flowed over us in a constant stream:
bad marriages, tragic burials,
childbirths, and olden times.

She took delight in her
grown grandsons who teased
her about peeking out the windows
to check on the neighbors,
and in her great-grandchildren
who were all clever and perfect.
She gathered us under her wings,
all Grandma Carrie's chicks.

Brothers and sisters: Lloyd, Ernie, Art, Harris, Mabel,
and Helen.

Uncle Ernie, an American hero.

American Hero

When you were eighteen years old
and a world away from Dakota,
out of the wheat fields, and into the steaming
jungles of the Philippines
where the enemy was trying to kill you,
were you scared, or just homesick?

When you came home exuberant with life,
and tried to tell about war the way it was,
the torture, the death, the suffering,
and your brothers could not
understand the horrors you saw,
were you frustrated, or just disappointed?

When you tried to forget and begin life
one step behind, seeking to drown the war
with love and family, and you had to go
from woman to woman, from family to family,
and the interior movie never ended,
were you just irresponsible, or a complete failure?

When you were older, worn out with searching
for peace, homeless, paranoid,
hiding in cornfields from imaginary agents,
no longer able to recognize
the love and concern of your family,
were you crazy, or just emotionally damaged?

When old age catches you in a veteran's home,
uncertain, medicated, struggling
to make a complete story of your life,
tended by strangers, mourned by your family,
will you find peace in life, or only in death?

No, Minnie wasn't that old; she was
wearing a centennial costume.

Grandma Brewer and one of her
great-grandchildren.

Minnie
(dedicated to my dear mother-in-law, Minnie Brewer)
March 19, 1916 - July 14, 2002

She was born into poverty
barely afloat on the backwater of society,
the family pet, that wolf at the door.

Although it was a chancy business,
she pinned all her hopes on a man,
as young women did in those days.
He was a hard worker, but life
had made him a bad drinker,
the bottle releasing furies in him
that could only be quelled by abuse.

So she left him; there was a divorce
at a time when that "just wasn't done."
She found herself alone,
three kids to support, no job,
no education, dependent
on the kindness of neighbors.

She met an unlikely Prince Charming,
a scrawny bachelor, hair thinning on top,
a worker, not a drinker.
He moved them off the mean streets.

They had two more children,
a chubby mischievous boy,
and, at long last, the little girl
she had so desperately longed for -
a buffer against all that boyish roughness.

She lived long and gently
surrounded by her family.
In her last days
she was tended night and day
by her loved ones
so she could die in her own bed,
which, by that time, was her only desire.

The Heart Place

They stand alone,
those four-square
white farm houses,
isolated on a neat
handkerchief of lawn.

Dwarfed by barns,
machine sheds,
towered over by
windmills and silos,
pressed by fields
of wheat and corn.

The houses were the heart
of the farm, the warmth,
the place where
dreams were formed.

The dreamers leave, though,
torn away by anticipation
of other lives.
The houses, no longer hearts
of anything, slowly
sag to ruin.

Part 2

My Dad Was a Real Farmer

Dad was a country boy.

Mom was a city girl.

Disparate Marriage

They met accidentally,
a city girl desperate to break
away from her volatile, abusive mother,
a country boy drawn eastward
from Dakota plains by the Great Depression,
worn down by the futility of growing wheat
to be stacked and burned in the fields.

He took her to live in the country,
called to farming
like a preacher called to his pulpit.
She learned to be a farm wife,
make gardens, milk cows, keep chickens,
always struggling to control things,
to be heard. Those were stormy years,
both bringing the defenses of abusive homes
to bargain on the table of love.

Three kids and four rented farms later,
they bought their own piece of land,
sand, shale, big barn, tiny make-do
house, a desperate need for cash.
She went back to school for a teaching certificate,
slid into teaching with a click of recognition.
She was not called to farming.

Their lives ran on parallel tracks,
hers in school, his in the fields,
always looking for common ground.
They have found it now, lie together,
differences buried under
a common stone.

Everybody needs lots of cousins!

Farm Kitchen
(in three parts)
Part I

Enter the fine, fragrant farm kitchen.
Open doors draw people in to
the warmth of the huge iron range,
to warm cold backsides against the reservoir,
to bathe tots on the warm oven door.
Boiled coffee blackens in a big tin pot,
thick and biting as acid.
Small talk rises above shrieks of children.
Pans bubble, hiss, and spatter.
The conductor of this chaos
waves her dripping wooden spoon,
choreographs family life.

Part 2

I stand on the open oven door wrapped in waves of gentle heat, wriggling impatiently under the rough washcloth, and the firm hand of my mother.

I am five years old, proud (haughty even) with the delight of going to school. My sister, small, round, ruddy as an apple, sits on the floor near the stove, playing like a baby with dolls. I am too old for dolls; I know how to read!

I don't remember what Alice is prattling about, but I am scornful. "You are such a baby. You can't even read! You don't even know what two plus two is."

Mother tightens her grip on my arm, gives me a sharp shake, is about to utter a reproof when Alice pipes up, "I do, too!" she declares firmly. "Two plus two is four!"

Mother laughs at me. I brood on the wisdom of sharing knowledge.

Eva and her cousins today.

Part 3

Sunday Dinner on the Farm

The men talk outside. Leaning, squatting, pacing, they debate the issues of the day, talk politics, and crops, drink lemonade, and fan themselves with wide straw hats.

The murmur of male voices drifts through the wide-open windows punctuated by the high, light voices of the women working in the steaming kitchen to get dinner ready.

Potatoes bubble to mealiness on the hot wood stove. Coffee, the original aromatherapy, perks at the back.
Big skillets of spring chickens, their lives laid down for the occasion, crisp up in deep sizzling lard. Warm pies cool on the cupboard.

My aunts step in and out carrying silverware and good china to the fully-extended dining room table. Pitchers of milk, ranks of dill pickles, plates of fresh bread are carried in, sacrifices on the altar of family togetherness.

Children circle underfoot, driven to ravenous hunger by the fragrance of the food. "Not now!" "Don't touch!" "Go outside!" A litany of rejection from pre-occupied mothers. Bits of gossip are whispered in passing. "Little pitchers have big ears," the warning cry as the children draw near.

The meal is ready. The men file through the hot kitchen wiping their brows. They take their places at the table and fix wiggling children with stern eyes. The women bring the hot food and slip into their chairs.

They bow their heads.

Dad in barn doorway.

Winter Milking

Open heavy doors, top half, bottom half.
Inside warmth, cavernous space,
neat rows of cows, breathing moistly, rhythmically.
Odor, a physical force, ammonia bite of urine,
sour whiff of silage, dusty, nose-tickling hay.

Crude wooden stool, worn smooth with repetition,
forehead rests on warm bovine flank.
Grasp warm leathery teats,
establish the rhythm.
Milk foams in pail, ringing stream on metal.

Barn cats sit, Egyptian sculptures,
attention fixed unwaveringly on white ambrosia.
Rise, pail full, pulling
stream of cats toward milk can, empty dish.

Calves blat and suck at pails of chalky milk replacer,
tongues rough as sand paper, frantic bumping heads,
blind seeking for nourishment.

Satisfaction reigns. Cows depleted,
calves repleted, cats completed,
delicately licking whiskers.
Chores are done, back out into the icy air.

Bringing in the hay wasn't nearly so exciting in later years. In the 60's Grandma Grabow, Eva, Kathy, Gene and little Gene brought in the last load of hay .

Last Load In

July afternoon air
like warm milk against the skin.
Thunder mutters in the distance.
Storm clouds tower in the west.

Last load of hay comes in from the field.
Horses lift dinner plate hooves,
puffs of dust, jangle of harness.

Uncle Ed looks out the hayloft door.
He has been mowing back,
spreading the hay evenly.

The wagon pulls up below the hayloft door.
Old Sally, the pulley horse,
has been dozing in the shade.
She shakes herself and moves forward.
Junior grabs her bridle
and backs her to the single tree.

The iron claws of the hayfork drop
down from the track above the hayloft door.
They can pick up half
a wagon load of hay at a time.
Pa sets the tines deep in the hay,
signals Junior who urges Old Sally forward.
In one magical motion the hay lifts,
wisps dropping, hits the track with a clang,
and disappears into the hayloft door.

Pa gathers the wisps and throws them
over the fence to the curious cows.
Junior puts the horses away.
The storm is overhead. Uncle Ed
tilts his face to the rain
and lets it wash away the chaff.

Eva's dad.

My Dad Was a Real Farmer

A real farmer has a calling
like a pastor or a doctor.
I am not talking now
of thousand acre farms,
of giant tractors
with air-conditioned cabs,
of diggers so wide they
wing up on the sides
to go down the road.

No, I am speaking
of a few sand and shale acres,
of tractors from
another era, of horse-drawn
machinery converted
by patience and ingenuity
to be pulled behind.

I am speaking
of constant oiling
and greasing,
of making parts from tin cans,
of holding everything
together with baling wire.

I am speaking of love
that touched everything
in his life -- wife, children,
neighbors; and the animals
he raised with affection
and butchered in the fall.

Uncle Harvey was in
the navy, and Uncle
Ralph, Uncle Bill,
Uncle Jack, and Uncle
Earl were in the army.
The homefront waited
in stillness to hear
from them.

World War II

Across the sea
bombs fell, men died,
towns passed into desolation.

My family was connected
to the war only by
staticky radio waves,
"This is Edward R.
Murrow reporting
from London. . ."

We were connected by
small fragile airmail
letters folded over
themselves to make
an envelope. Short
assurances that when
that letter left their hand,
beloved sons and brothers
were alive and yearning for home.

Mommy took our ration
books to town,
tore perforated stamps off,
traded them for sugar or shoes.

Daddy rolled his own,
tapping tobacco into
crinkly papers, magically
twirling it into a cigarette.

I saved pennies,
took ten to school on Fridays
tied up in the corner of a hanky.
Dreamed sticky thoughts
of the candy I could have had.
I bought a liberty stamp,
carefully pasted it into
a special book. A full book
was traded for a savings bond.
Did I ever fill a whole book?

I saved tinfoil, carefully
pealing it off gum wrappers,
and the inside of
cigarette packs, pressing
it into a large ball.

One fall our country school
gathered milkweed pods,
brown gunny sacks full.
The seedy silk inside
the pods stuffed life vests.
Real soldiers came
in a big army truck,
thanked us, and took
our bags away to war.

War slides along
the peripheral vision
of a child - just
another grown-up thing.
I would not know what
war really was until I was
old enough to feel
it in my heart.

No, I wasn't on a
starvation diet. I had
been in the hospital
for eight weeks.

Summer of '44

My bed floated
on the leafy tree-top
outside my window.
I could see the roof
of the hospital annex.
Mourning doves paced there,
the haunting sadness
of their song reminding
me of water. I was by turn
feverish and lethargic,
spoiled and cranky.
I was eight years old,
and I wanted to go home.

Soldiers on the battlefield
were kept alive with sulfa
pills and penicillin, and so was I.
My parents came everyday,
but my most constant
companion was a small
rag doll. She endured
everything, frantic
clutching, nasty-tempered
pinches, even being thrown
across the room. The hospital
staff worked tirelessly
to keep me amused, to keep
me connected to life.

Six weeks of sulfa pills
to stabilize the infection,
an operation to remove
my burst appendix, two
weeks of recovery, and it
was all over - a life-changing
experience. I was
stick-thin, weak for a time;
then life was back to normal.

How would my life have
been different without
that double assault on my body?
Without the indignity of illness?
Without the trauma of surgery?
Is that where I learned to
drift through life trying
not to let anything
touch me too deeply?

Different boys, different cars. These two are looking for a ride.

Song of the Fifties

When I was a girl,
boys had cars
so they could go places.
Girls didn't have cars,
but they had boyfriends
so they could go places.

The ability of mobility
wasn't free.
Girls were expected
to pay for their rides.

Insistent boys
kissed them roughly,
touched them intimately,
sometimes took them
to places they
weren't prepared to go.

But what was a girl to do?
Boys had the power;
boys had the cars.

All dressed up (above).
Check out the hairdo (below).

Friday Night Fashion

The gym, a wall of solid sound,
young and old screaming
as though the act of exhortation
would result in scores.

Cheerleaders, bouncing, twirling,
chanting, "Two, four, six, eight,
who do we appreciate. . ."

I, in my fashionable, brown circle skirt,
swaying to the rhythm of the chants,
more excited about my own appearance
than the outcome of the game.

Last Dance

Dust floats from stomping feet. My heart throbs in rhythm to the drum and bass. I shrink back against the wall . . . alone for
Goodnight Ladies . . . trying not to look as conspicuous and embarrassed as I feel. A stir by the door where the young men smoke and gossip. One of them, the one I have a secret crush on, white t-shirt flashing against tan throat, older, so cool, toes out his cigarette on the floor, walks toward me. We dance. I breathe him in, the smell of Old Spice, cigarettes, a hint of barn. His hand is calloused and warm.

No matter that he will soon go off to war, that he will die, that I will marry, have children, live a whole lifetime of never dancing. This will be a moment to treasure.

Yearning

I spent my youth as freely as the Prodigal Son,
tossed away the years with abandon.
I let the music take me and danced
as thoughtlessly as the grasshopper.
I looked at the elderly with hard eyes
and thought, I will never be like that!

Now the years are gone, and I am old,
invisible as the old are, my eyes resting
on the bleak landscape of my life.
But, deep inside, I still hear the music,
and Oh! I want to dance!

All dressed up and nowhere to go!

Betrayal

Once there was a girl who
gave up her childhood
for adult things.
She no longer dug
caves in the sand bank
or cut out paper dolls
with her sister.
She wore lipstick,
and looked at boys
through different eyes.

Her world sparkled
like a dew-dropped
spider web. It was a web,
of course, and soon
she was stuck fast,
rolled in the webbed
cocoon of adulthood.
She was trapped between
never being a child again
and never being a butterfly.

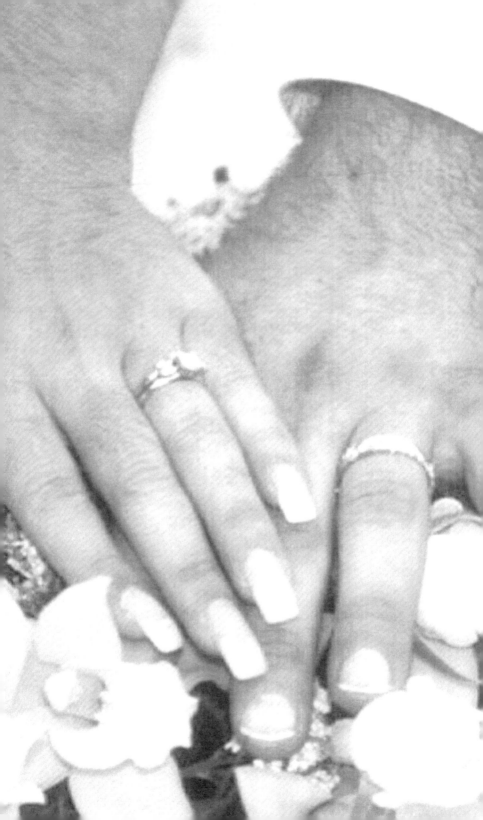

Part 3

It Might Have Been

A Love Story

Pay attention! This is my love story.
In the 50's two kids got married.
He was happy; he had someone
to do chores and boss around.
She was happy; she had a husband
and a wedding ring, in the 50's
all a girl needed to be a success.

Then the drift began.
They had nothing in common.
She would rather read than cook
or clean. He would rather hunt
and fish than come home.
The conflicts arising were mostly
silent battles of will and stubbornness,
the explosions infrequent but devastating.

They rattled along together
until the 90's when a tumor
ate him up. Then she realized
she had not lost her best friend,
but her best enemy --
and it hurt just as much.

Gardening is my favorite summer activity.

Let Summer Be My Love

Woo me not with silver songs
of dancing snowflakes,
of fields wind-sculpted
into icy drifts . . .
    but sing to me of summer

wrapped in air as warm
and gentle as a lover's kiss.
Delight my eye with hummingbirds,
with graceful swaying lilies.

Perfume the air with scent of roses,
the sweet musk of petunias,
the spicy smell of marigolds,
with breezes blowing
over fields of new mown hay.

Let the cool liquid call
of the mourning dove
wake me from my slumbers,
and the pulsing trill of tree frogs
lull me to my dreams.

River on a Summer Evening

In the heat of the evening,
hand in hand
we walk slowly to the river.

Bodies sun-burned,
prickly with hay chaff,
wrapped in wet flannel air.

From the dusky woods
we hear the river murmur
over the sand bar.

We sink into the sluggish current,
let the amber water flow over us
taking the sweat, the pain.

We walk back through the woods,
sink down on fleshy emerald grasses,
and give our bodies to each other
as we gave them to the river.

Lovers As Aztecs

We are both conquered
and conquistadors.
We explore one another,
mapping all of the hidden places.

We cut the living heart
from our beloved,
eat the dripping organ,
not for cruelty,
but to be one with a sacred object.

We stand aghast
with bloodied chin
wondering why our love is dead.

Bells are ringing - round one.

It Might Have Been

Of all sad words
of tongue and pen,
the saddest are these,
what might have been.

So young, so ill-at-ease
in all their finery,
they stand to say their vows.
At that moment
wrapped in tender surety
their love will last from now. . .
          until forever. . .

They take love off to live
in cramped apartments,
work so hard and never get ahead.
They grind love down between
their iron wills till tarnished,
ragged, almost dead.

They never think
to shine it on a Sunday.
They only think my way
or none! They smolder
lonely and detached.
Love drifts away.

They reach old age,
and love is far behind them.
Scar tissue binds them
from a thousand wounds
inflicted on each other
in that lifetime since
they were loving bride and groom.

First Apartment

The lobby reeks of cooking food
and diaper pails.
The apartment is three small, dark
rooms with walls of cardboard,
furnished with a chipped-enamel
gas range and a refrigerator,
rusty stain sliding down the door.

We have a bed and a TV set,
the opium of the poor.
I sink into soap operas.
No one in Another World shouts,
comes home drunk,
slaps kids around.
In that world women sniffle
discreet tears while handsome
lovers hold them gently. No ghastly
wracking sobs at midnight.

I, the new wife,
first time in squalid city,
feel my known world tremble underfoot,
feel my defenses slip,
feel the heartbreak coming.

It Has Always Looked Half-Furnished

We were young,
no money.
The apartment
came with
chipped-enamel gas stove,
old refrigerator,
rusty stain down its door.

His mother gave us
a wobbly table
and two chairs.
They didn't even match.
How could we have company?

The problem kept me
from hanging curtains,
framing pictures,
planning menus,
giving all of myself.
Half-furnished --
half-life.

Dream House

I have always built castles in the air,
ethereal homes, golden with sunlight,
open to spring-scented breezes.

I furnished my castles
with fragile, exquisite things,
nothing hand-me-down,

secondhand, worn, ugly.
My castles were ruled by love;
peace and harmony prevailed.

No one was angry, shouted
cruel wounding words;
the doors would not slam shut.

No one cried in my castles;
they were built of dreams.
How I wish I could have lived there!

Jessica

Emily

All the babies
I fell for.

Chris

Kathy

Carmen

Clay

Gene

Trey

I Fell for You, Babe

Even though I carried you
tucked under my heart
for nine long months,

even though the doctor
said I would have a baby,
and we planned for
and spoke of a baby,

even though other mothers-
in-waiting discussed
breast feeding and colic,
and gushed of their love
for their babies,

I could not picture
a baby in my life.
I could not imagine
the look of you,
the feel of you in my arms.

Then one day there you were,
the nurse presenting you
like a treasure wrapped
in receiving blankets.
How did my arms know
exactly how to cradle you
against my breast?

I imagined a click
as you settled into
that place in my heart
reserved unknowingly
for you. It was love
at first sight; it will be
love forever.

Reading has always been my favorite activity.

The Library at Kenosha

I hurry up the marble steps,
arms clasped around books,
heart pounding, joy rising,
and step into the vaulted silence.
I want to take off my shoes
for this is my sacred ground.

The library, dim and hushed,
is full of murmurous voices.
Sharper sounds echo softly.

Rows and rows of bookshelves.
Thousands of doorways to distant
places, other times, endless
escapes from my everyday sameness.

This is an oasis for my soul.
Arms full of different books,
running lightly down the stairs,
my feet hardly touch the ground.

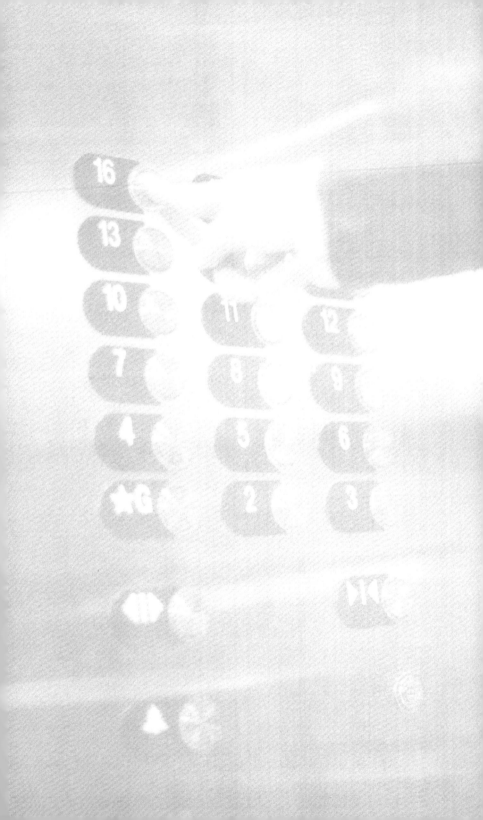

Accepting Cash or Credit Cards

Life is like a department store
elevator - up and down, up
and down. From sub-basements
to lofty furniture salesrooms,
the doors slide open on vast
expanses of merchandise.

I leave the elevator tentatively,
run my fingers over the dazzling
display of lifestyles,
consider patterns, shapes, and forms.
I try on one persona and then
another, surround myself
with classics or punk chic.

Shopping for a life
is exhausting.
In the end everything
is too expensive.

Good and Better

I have weighed two hundred pounds
and lived in a "mobile" home,
fixed hamburger four nights a week,
washed and ironed every stitch the family wore.

I have run up clothes on the sewing machine,
darned socks, mended knees on jeans,
baked cookies, cakes, casseroles, pies,
and loaves of bread by the half dozen.

I have done the stoop-work of gardening
bending, planting, weeding, harvesting.
I have canned tomatoes in August
when the humidity was so intense,
it was like breathing underwater.

I have cleaned my house thoroughly
every Friday so it looked good for the weekend,
and sat down in the mess on Monday
and read all day long without a qualm.

I have lived poor, and I have lived better,
and I am here to tell you
that there is no shame in being poor,
but there is great joy in living better!

A spiral
through my life.

We Carry It All

Like the chambered nautilus
we carry our past lives with us.
Hardened chambers spiral

through our sub-conscious.
The first cribs of our sentient
being where our cries

were answered or not.
The childhood rooms cluttered
with sibling rivalries,

the opening spaces of young adulthood.
The cramped, raggedy rooms
of early marriage, the wide

bustling rooms of maternity,
the wild vastness
of working in the outside world.

Calcified, densely packed,
crimping here, stretching there,
bearing down ever more
heavily as we age.

Part 4

Who Folded This Map, Anyway?

East is east; west is west; home is best.

From My Window

I see
porch railing,
driveway,
road,
ribbon of
blacktop between
white shoulders.

Railroad tracks,
gentle roll of fields
fallow so long
pine trees show their points
above the grasses,
tawny gold, tan, and darker brown,
on and on until my eye
runs smack!
into the woods along the river.

Black-green pines,
splashes of rust where
oak leaves cling tenaciously
to ice-slick limbs.
The lacy mesh of a thousand
branches waiting
to be touched by the sun,
to burst into leaf.

Ordinary in the extreme,
but burned onto my retina
so that when my eye touches it,
and the components slide into place,
I know I am home.

Mother always knew where I
was coming from.

Unspoken, But Heard

I never said, "I love you"
to my mother
although she was three years
dying, and I had ample time.

I was married, a working
mother of teen-agers,
a frantic, harried, poor
caregiver. As time went by,
she became the child,
I the mother.

In the grey dawn we sat
in her hospital room
waiting for the amputation
of the foot that wouldn't heal.
I, sitting on my hands
so she wouldn't have to
reprimand me for biting
my nails. She, staring
quietly at the ceiling.

"Are you afraid?" I asked.
"No," she said. "I am not
afraid." Because I could
not find the words I wanted
to say, I blurted out, "I wish
you had someone more comforting
to be with you." She
turned her head and smiled,
"That's okay. I know where
you are coming from."

You couldn't go
wrong with a
county guy.

Life in a Drawer

There are one hundred twenty-six
items in this drawer.
It was my husband's
hoarding place, and fifteen years
later it is little disturbed.
The essence of the man is there,
small, useless, mysterious pieces
beyond my understanding.

Gobs of sticky, rusted keys.
He thought keys were power,
keys to places he didn't belong,
keys to unopened doors,
now keys to unknown doors.

Screwdrivers, pliers, wrenches,
thirty different tools, large and small.
Decks of cards. He loved to play
cards at the bar, if winning.

Single shoelace, dried tubes
of glue, a black crayon,
clusters of small screws,
sunglasses, nail clippers,
aquarium sealer, jackknife,
superball, suction cups
to hang suncatchers, a wooden
drink token from a bar long gone.

A drawer full of flotsam saved
by a man who was raised with
nothing and never intended
to go there again.

Midnight in the Temperate Zone

Day-heat lingers.
Flat metal disc of moon is
pinned to purple-black sky.
Fireflies glimmering
in black shade
mirror stars above.
Sleepy murmuring of
birds has died away.
Pulsing song of tree frogs
accentuates stillness,

Off on the hill
coyotes raise their
voices in songs
to the moon,
yip and warble mournfully.
My breath quickens.
My belly tightens.
I want to join
their lonely song.

The Woman Who Lost Things

Once there was a woman who lost things.
She lost her keys and earrings,
receipts and small change.
She lost her father suddenly
on an April afternoon,
and her mother after three hard

years of digging in and hanging on.
She even lost her husband
before his time, but that may
not have been completely accidental.
You would think that was enough to lose,
but, no, she lost grandchildren, friends,

mentors, and wonderful teachers.
You would think such a careless
woman would try to mend her ways
and stop losing such precious things.
She would, but now she feels
that she is losing herself.

I was gonna be a cowgirl.

Who Folded This Map, Anyway?

Here I am at the Last Resort
on the shores of Dire Straits
between a rock and a hard place.

It is not exactly what I
planned for life.
I was headed for Shangri--La,

high in the mountains,
rarified air, golden dreams,
but I took a wrong turn somewhere,

wound up in high anxiety instead.
Driving with a faulty map,
Utopia was merely useless;

Heaven was really Hell.
But, let's face it, it could be worse.
It's not crowded here. Nobody

is telling me what to do,
and I am still a couple
of miles from old age.

With a hat like that, who
needs a perm?

Get a Perm

I'm getting into a rut here,
fading fast. Need to perk up.
Maybe my hair . . . No dye.
I hate those funky ends showing up.
I could get a perm . . .
some bouncy curls
wouldn't be all bad.

I had a perm once,
got lots of metal curlers
all over my head,
got hooked up to a big machine,
got my head baked!
Made my hair all frizzy,
burnt the ends,
but, my! wasn't I the living end!

I was twelve at the time,
felt movie-star gorgeous
at the very thought of that cloud
of crispy hair floating
on top of my head.

If I was all curly and cute,
I might get a man.
Think about that!
Well . . . maybe not a perm.

Even in our
differences,
we were
together.

My Mother's Eyes

I have my mother in my head now.
I look out through her judgmental eyes,
washed blue like mine, but so strict.

She speaks with my tongue,
black, humorless words
that shrivel dreams and make hope hopeless.

She needed those defenses
against the dark abuses of her childhood,
needed to keep others in that cool,
blue area beyond intimacy.

She has been gone for twenty years,
and still she clamors in my mind,
"Don't". . . "You'll never". . . "I'm right!"

While I am here she will never be forgotten.
If only I could get her from my head
to my arms and rock her until
her world was rainbow.

The Woman Who Loved a Horse

A woman, confined to her room, had a horse for a neighbor. From her window she could see the horse in its small pasture. The horse had been a gift for a young girl who had lost interest in it.

The woman saw the horse standing alone, head drooping. The horse ate alone, drank alone, and ran about its enclosure alone. No one spoke to, admired, or caressed the horse. The woman felt very sad for the lonely horse.

The woman looked around her. She was eating her lunch alone, drinking her coffee alone. She had no one to admire her and certainly no one to caress her. She and the horse were kindred spirits.

More and more as she watched the horse, the woman imagined herself talking gently to the horse, feeding it carrots and sugar cubes. She could see herself braiding the horse's pale mane and tail, threading the plaits with ribbon. She felt herself sitting on the sleek brown horse, animal warmth and muscles rippling under her thighs. She could feel the wind on her face, lifting her hair as they galloped freely over the fields.

No one else saw the relationship the woman had with the horse, saw how her spirit attended the horse, how the horse filled her life. Sometimes, after her children had stopped briefly to visit, they left saying, "Mother doesn't really seem to be present today." But they never bothered to find out where she was.

The Bone Singer
(after Clarissa Pinkola Estes)

Some days I feel fragmented,
strewn across the landscape.
I need the Bone Singer,

the old hag of legends,
who shuffles along desert paths
collecting bones . . .

bones of her totem animal, the wolf.
She lays them out on the hot sand,
completes each skeleton,

then she lifts her fleshy arms and sings,
low vibrant humming,
rising, rising in crescendo,

until the earth shudders,
the air booms, the bones
are clothed in flesh and fur,

and the wolf runs free.
I dream myself into the bones
of the wolf. I shudder with the earth

as her voice booms around me.
I will be made whole.
I can run free.

Summer of '06

Once there was a woman who could not walk. Sometimes she worried about that. Suppose there was a tornado? She imagined sliding down the cellar stairs to safety but could not quite imagine arriving in a safe place.

Luckily she had a chair with wheels. It went quite well on the tiled floor but was very hard to propel across the carpet. "This must be good for my abs," the woman thought as she jerked herself along using her one good leg, although, being a fat woman, she had no idea where her "abs" were.

She read a lot, did crossword puzzles, and played games on her computer. She dreamed of getting in her car and driving away, but her children had parked the car across the yard. She napped a lot because when she was asleep she didn't feel like she was missing her life.

Her horoscope this week says it is good for her to take a backseat and let herself be guided. She wishes the stars would guide her somewhere else.

The Older I Get, the More Things Change

They say the climate is changing.
They say the glaciers are melting
in the north country.
They say when we destroy
habitat, species disappear.
They say polar bears roam
aimlessly looking for ice.

They say honeybees
are disappearing.
The hives stand empty.

This is bad news;
bees have a keen
intelligence
perhaps surpassing our own.

They communicate
complex directions to nectar-
laden flowers. They don't
cheat, steal, make war.
They make it possible
for man to grow food.

So where have they gone?
Are they being beamed up
to pollinate orchards
in an alien world?

Is it an apian suicide pact?
Have they given up in despair?
Are we really spreading
so much poison over the land
we are killing the creatures
we need the most?
Is this a sign of end times?
Maybe I have been around too long!

Selective Memory

I don't remember much anymore,
    not all of the state capitols,
    not where I put my pen,
    not the scent of Evening In Paris
    (although I do remember it was my mother's favorite perfume),
    not the exact shade of my father's brown hair.
I barely remember the clenching thrill deep in my belly
    when my husband's hand touched me.
    Oh, that was so long ago . . . I almost
    remember how good it felt later
    when he rubbed my back in slow circles
    and whispered, "Rest now, rest."
    I don't remember when he left.
I do remember when I had a name.
    Sometimes it was Mommy, sometimes Gram,
    sometimes it was Eva, spoken tenderly.
    I don't remember where I lost it.
The nurses here call me Dear.
    "Move over, Dear; that's a good girl,"
    I remember talking to my dog like that.
    I don't remember that dog's name . . .
The nurses here have cold stethoscopes
    and the smell of sterile solutions about them.
    They touch quickly and competently.
    "Good morning," they say brightly. "Do
    you remember my name this morning?"
    And sometimes I do,
And sometimes I won't!

Eva at two
and her
little dog
Scottie.

Woman on the Edge of Age

At seventy:
I have more past than future,
more memory than anticipation,
more nostalgia than excitement,
more regrets than triumphs.

It is a time to reflect on life,
to embrace the joys,
touch gently on the sorrows,
call up the faces of loves I have lost. . .
so many faces by this time.

At times a great anger rises in me,
for the unlovely child I was,
for the reluctant wife,
the confused young mother.

"Give me back my life," I cry.
"Let me do it over and get it right!"
So I may have some wisdom
to carry with me when I step
off the edge of age.

My little
dog and I
have come
full circle.

Writing Is . . .

Writing is long periods of befuddlement followed by short bursts of terror. There is something profound to say, but can I pull it out of my heart without damaging the muscle?

Ah-h, at last I have the words down on paper. Perfectly formed sentences made up of graceful and witty phrases. I read them over and glow with satisfaction -- perfection!

The next day I read it again. I am appalled! What a piece of junk! I scream, pull out my hair, cross out passive verbs, cliches, whole dead sentences. I wad the paper up to throw it away, but WAIT . . . I see a good sentence, a pleasing phrase. I type them in and begin again.

Many hours later I have a fair piece of work. The next day it seems the same. I breathe a sigh of relief. I have written well.

About the Author

Eva Mewes lives in a small town in west central Wisconsin. She began seriously writing poetry after retiring. She has had poems published in the Wisconsin Poet's Calendar and two small chapbooks, *Musings* and *Glimpses*.

This book could be called realism filtered through poetic imagination and shouldn't be taken for the whole truth.